1

The UFC is an American mixed martial arts (MMA) organization that was founded in 1993.

It is currently the largest MMA promoter in the world, and its events are broadcast worldwide.

The UFC has been one of the main drivers behind the growth and popularity of MMA worldwide.

In UFC events, fighters compete in an octagon (an enclosed area with an octagonal shape) using a combination of stand-up and ground fighting techniques.

Fighters can use strikes, kicks, knees, elbows, grappling, and takedowns to try to defeat their opponent.

Fights usually have a duration of three to five rounds, and the winner is determined by knockout, submission, judges' decision, or opponent's disqualification.

The UFC has different weight categories, ranging from flyweight (up to 56.7 kg) to heavyweight (over 120.2 kg).

Fighters must adhere to certain rules and safety requirements, including regular medical examinations and the prohibition of certain types of strikes.

The UFC has seen many famous and successful fighters over the years, including Conor McGregor, Georges St-Pierre, Anderson Silva, Jon Jones, Khabib Nurmagomedov, Ronda Rousey, and many more.

The organization has also faced criticism for its violence and lack of regulation in its early years, and has worked to improve fighter safety and the public image of MMA as a whole.

101

STRANGE BUT TRUE

UFC FACTS

2

Since its foundation in 1993, the UFC has experienced impressive growth.

Currently, the UFC is the largest MMA promoter in the world and is broadcast in over 150 countries worldwide, reaching millions of viewers.

The sport's popularity has grown so much that the UFC has organized events in diverse locations such as Abu Dhabi, Moscow, Sydney, and Las Vegas, to name just a few.

In addition to live event broadcasts, the UFC has also developed a strong online presence.

Its YouTube channel has over 11 million subscribers and 3.5 billion views, reflecting the large number of people following the organization worldwide.

The UFC has also been able to attract a large number of talented fighters from different parts of the world.

Currently, the UFC has over 400 fighters from 30 different nationalities under contract, demonstrating the diversity and global reach of the sport.

The growth of the UFC has been so remarkable that the organization has had a significant impact on popular culture.

MMA has been the subject of numerous documentaries, TV shows, and movies, and many UFC fighters have become stars on the big and small screens.

3

Requirements and Basic Equipment.

-Octagon: Although many people think it is for making the show more sadistic by enclosing two fighters in a cage, the truth is quite the opposite. It is always about ensuring the safety of the fighter, as taking the fight to the ground could result in falling outside, which is prevented by the cage.

-Gloves and hand wraps: They must be approved by the commission regulating the event, weighing 4 ounces (113 grams), and have open fingers to allow for gripping. The hand wraps should be soft gauze fabric with the appropriate measurements and must be applied in the presence of the commission and the opponent's corner manager.

-Mouthguards: Approved by the responsible doctor. If the mouthguard unintentionally shifts during the fight, the referee must stop the bout.

-Attire: The use of footwear or any type of foot wrapping is prohibited. T-shirts are only allowed for female fighters.

-Time limit and rounds: Regular fights consist of three rounds. All title or main event fights are scheduled for five rounds with a duration of five minutes per round and one minute of rest between them.

-Anti-doping tests: Random testing is conducted in accordance with state or country regulations without restrictions.

4

UFC Weight Categories and Current Champions.

- Strawweight (female) up to 115 pounds (52 kg)

- Flyweight up to 125 pounds or less (56.7 kg or less)

- Bantamweight from 125 to 135 pounds (56.7 to 61.2 kg)

- Featherweight from 135 to 145 pounds (61.2 to 65.7 kg)

- Lightweight from 145 to 155 pounds (65.7 to 70.3 kg)

- Welterweight from 155 to 170 pounds (70.3 to 77.1 kg)

- Middleweight from 170 to 185 pounds (77.1 to 83.9 kg)

- Light heavyweight from 185 to 205 pounds (83.9 to 92.9 kg)

- Heavyweight from 205 to 265 pounds (92.9 to 120.2 kg)

5

People who are unfamiliar with this sport often tend to label the spectacle as something violent, where anything goes and the sole purpose is seeking thrills, drawing a certain similarity to gladiator fights in the Roman Colosseum.

However, despite its origins in "Vale Tudo," there are rules in place to protect the fighters and ensure their safety.

Strikes to dangerous areas (such as the back of the head, spine, genitals, etc.) are prohibited, as well as manipulating small joints (fingers), biting, poking fingers in the eyes, or engaging in other "dirty actions" more typical of a street fight.

6

How can a bout end?

-Knockout (K.O.): This is what every fighter aims for, as it is not only the most spectacular but also gets the fans out of their seats. It occurs when a fighter becomes unconscious, disoriented, or unable to defend themselves.

-Technical knockout (TKO): The referee stops the fight due to lack of response and/or defense from one of the fighters.

-Submission: A fighter causes their opponent to surrender or lose consciousness through a chokehold or joint lock. This type of finish is often seen as requiring more skill and strategy.

-Unanimous decision: All three judges agree on the winner.

-Split decision: Two judges choose the same winner, while the third judge selects the other fighter.

-Majority decision: Two judges agree on the same winner, and the third judge calls it a draw.

-Majority draw: Two judges declare a draw, while the third judge chooses a winner.

-Technical draw: This occurs when a fighter cannot continue the bout due to an accidental injury caused by an illegal strike from the opponent, such as an eye or groin injury. In this case, the result of the fight is determined by the rules of the state or country where the event takes place.

7

UFC fighters are athletes who have dedicated many years of effort and sacrifice to become professional fighters.

Many of them compete in smaller competitions to improve and expand their striking styles until they reach the holy grail of organizations: the UFC.

They train many hours a week, making it a full-time job, and their training includes sparring sessions to prepare specific strategies depending on the upcoming fight.

Recovery after fights and training is crucial.

Doctors determine how much time they need to rest before their next fight based on the intensity of the fight, including bruises, injuries, and fractures.

8

The company Zuffa, led by the Fertitta brothers, purchased the UFC in 2001 for a relatively modest amount of $2 million.

At that time, the UFC was in a financially difficult situation, and the sport was not as popular as it is today.

The new owners, headed by Dana White, invested a lot of time and money in promoting the UFC and improving the rules and safety of the sport.

Over time, the popularity of the UFC grew, and it became one of the most significant and profitable sports in the world.

In 2016, WME-IMG acquired the UFC from Zuffa for the astonishing sum of $4 billion, making it one of the largest transactions in sports history.

Despite the change in ownership, Dana White continued to lead the organization and has helped maintain its popularity and growth worldwide.

9

In the UFC, only one belt is awarded to each champion in each weight category.

The belt represents the champion's recognition as the best fighter in their respective weight division and is a symbol of achievement in the sport.

The belts are made of leather and 24-karat gold plating, often including diamonds and other gemstones.

The belts are personalized for each champion, with their name and weight division engraved in the center.

Some belts can weigh around 6 kilograms of pure gold, and they can sometimes cost hundreds of thousands of dollars due to the precious materials and craftsmanship used to create them.

It should be noted that, although champions are recognized with a belt, they are not required to carry it with them at every public appearance or event.

Many champions choose to wear it on special occasions or during award ceremonies.

Additionally, in the event of losing the title, the belt must be handed over to the new champion.

10

The UFC has faced criticism and regulations due to its violent nature.

In addition to Germany in 2010, some other countries have also banned or restricted the UFC in the past, such as China, France, and New York.

In some cases, these restrictions have been lifted after the UFC worked with authorities to comply with local regulations and improve fighter safety.

It is important to highlight that the UFC has implemented a series of safety measures to ensure the protection of fighters, including the mandatory use of padded gloves, the prohibition of certain dangerous strikes, and thorough medical testing before each fight.

Despite the criticism and regulations, the UFC has managed to gain great popularity worldwide and has become a multi-billion dollar company with a very loyal fan base.

Additionally, the UFC has made efforts to expand into new markets and attract new fans by organizing events in different parts of the world and signing fighters from various nationalities.

11

Sometimes, reality surpasses fiction.

The traditional video game franchise Mortal Kombat, distributed by Midway Games, may have served as inspiration for the UFC to design its battle arena in the shape of an octagon.

Other versions suggest that the divine inspiration didn't actually come from Mortal Kombat, but from Chuck Norris' movie "The Octagon," in which the former karate champion fought against five ninjas.

12

McGregor is the most media-driven fighter in UFC history.

The main reason for this status is that in 2015, he sent José Aldo to the canvas in just 13 seconds.

The fastest knockout actually belongs to Duane Ludwig, with a victory in 6 seconds in his record.

However, unlike the American, McGregor's victory in 2015 helped him become the unified champion of the UFC Featherweight Championship.

13

UFC 229, 2.4 million PPV sales.

UFC 194 was a highly anticipated event as it featured a championship fight between the then-featherweight champion José Aldo and the Irish challenger Conor McGregor.

The fight took place on December 12, 2015, in Las Vegas, Nevada. It was heavily promoted and anticipated, as both fighters were rising stars and had built a great rivalry leading up to the fight.

The fight between Aldo and McGregor ended spectacularly, with McGregor scoring an impressive knockout in just 13 seconds of the first round to become the new featherweight champion.

Although it was a short fight, it was very thrilling and managed to attract a large number of fans.

However, despite the significance and excitement surrounding UFC 194, it didn't surpass the PPV sales of UFC 229, which featured a fight between McGregor and Russian fighter Khabib Nurmagomedov.

UFC 229 also had significant promotion and advertising leading up to the event, and the rivalry between McGregor and Nurmagomedov was highly intense.

Additionally, the event had the controversial ending where there was a massive brawl in the octagon after Nurmagomedov won the fight by submission in the fourth round.

14

The significance that the UFC has gained, thanks to fights like McGregor and Nurmagomedov, has led to an unstoppable growth in the number of commercial partners for the premier mixed martial arts competition.

Litecoin and PokerStars were the last two companies to establish an alliance with the UFC in 2018.

The Litecoin agreement marked the first relationship with a virtual currency.

Meanwhile, PokerStars became the first Official Poker Partner in the history of the UFC brand.

15

Juan Espino was the first Spaniard to win a UFC fight.

There have been Americans, Russians, Brazilians, Irish, and now a Spaniard.

In the record books of a competition as multicultural as the UFC, the first victory of a Spanish fighter is already registered.

Juan Espino was born in 1980 in Las Palmas de Gran Canaria.

"El Guapo's" career has taken diverse paths, as his sporting beginnings came through Canarian wrestling, and he combined that discipline with others such as grappling, Korean ssireum, and jiu-jitsu.

His debut in the UFC took place when he defeated Justin Frazier.

16

In the early UFC events, there were not many rules. It was a mixed martial arts tournament that pitted fighters from different disciplines in fights with minimal restrictions.

The first event took place in November 1993, with the goal of determining which fighting style was the most effective.

At that time, participants could use any technique they wanted, and there were only three "honorable" rules that had to be followed: no biting, no striking the groin, and no eye gouging.

Additionally, gloves were optional, and fights had no time limit, so they could last until one of the fighters surrendered, was knocked out, or the referee decided to stop the fight.

Over time, the UFC has adopted a series of rules to make the fights safer and more sportsmanlike, and it has become an organization regulated by state athletic commissions.

17

Nate Diaz never faced Khabib Nurmagomedov in an official UFC fight.

What did happen was that after Khabib's victory over Conor McGregor at UFC 229, Nate Diaz taunted him on social media, which provoked a response from Khabib.

The two encountered each other at a UFC event and had a heated discussion that led to shoving and fights between their teams.

However, they never ended up fighting inside the octagon.

18

The rivalry between Jon Jones and Daniel Cormier developed over several years while both were UFC light heavyweight champions.

Their first scheduled fight, UFC 178 in 2014, had to be canceled due to an injury suffered by Jones.

They eventually faced off at UFC 182 in January 2015, where Jones won by unanimous decision.

Tension between the two continued on social media and at public events, and in 2016 they fought again at UFC 200 for the light heavyweight title, with Jones winning by unanimous decision.

However, shortly after, he was stripped of the title and suspended for doping.

In 2017, Cormier won the vacant light heavyweight title, and Jones returned from his suspension in 2018 to face him at UFC 214.

Jones won by knockout in the third round, but the fight was overturned after it was discovered that Jones tested positive for banned substances.

The tension between the two escalated at a pre-fight press conference for UFC 178, where Jones pushed Cormier, sparking a brawl between them.

They have also had verbal confrontations on social media and on television shows.

Despite the rivalry, both have expressed mutual respect and have spoken positively about each other on several occasions.

19

UFC Fight Night 218 on August 7, 2021, in Las Vegas featured a fight between Brazilian fighters Jessica Andrade and Cynthia Calvillo in the women's flyweight category.

Andrade managed to submit Calvillo with an arm triangle in the first round, securing the victory by submission.

Andrade, nicknamed "Bate Estaca," is a Brazilian fighter with a long career in the UFC.

She had previously competed in the strawweight category and had won the championship in that division.

Currently, she is in the flyweight category and holds a prominent position in the division's rankings.

Calvillo, on the other hand, is a Mexican-American fighter who has been competing in the UFC since 2017.

She has also fought in the women's strawweight category and is currently in the flyweight category.

This fight was one of the many thrilling contests that have taken place in the UFC over the years.

The UFC is known for presenting some of the most exciting and challenging fights in the world of mixed martial arts.

20

Bonuses are a financial incentive awarded by the UFC to fighters who have had an outstanding performance in an event.

These bonuses are given in three categories: "Fight of the Night," "Performance of the Night," and sometimes "Knockout of the Night" or "Submission of the Night."

In this case, at the event where Andrade and Lemos fought, two "Performance of the Night" bonuses were awarded to Jéssica Andrade and Claudio Puelles, and a "Fight of the Night" bonus was given to Sergey Khandozhko and Dwight Grant.

Each fighter received a bonus of $50,000 for their performance.

These bonuses can vary from event to event and can serve as an additional incentive for fighters to give their best effort in the octagon.

21

The virus caused withdrawals.

Unfortunately, it is common for fighters to have to withdraw from a fight due to injuries or illnesses, and in this case, Louis Cosce tested positive for COVID-19 and couldn't compete in the bout against Preston Parsons.

As a result, Parsons had to face a last-minute replacement, Evan Elder, in the welterweight category.

Elder, who had a record of 3 wins and 1 loss in his professional career, ended up losing by submission in the second round against Parsons.

It was a missed opportunity for Cosce and a significant victory for Parsons in his UFC debut.

22

Bosnian fighter Damir Hadžović is a professional mixed martial artist (MMA) who competes in the lightweight category.

Hadžović has competed in various MMA organizations, including the UFC, where he has faced notable opponents in his division.

In 2021, Hadžović was scheduled to fight American fighter Steve Garcia in an MMA bout in the United States.

However, the fight could not take place due to visa issues for Hadžović.

In order to enter the United States and compete in an MMA event, foreign fighters must obtain a work visa that allows them to work legally in the country.

Obtaining a visa can be a lengthy and complicated process that may require extensive documentation and meeting certain requirements.

In Hadžović's case, it is unclear what specific problems he had with his visa.

It is possible that his application was denied due to documentation issues or because he did not meet certain requirements.

In any case, his inability to obtain a visa left him unable to compete in the fight against Steve Garcia.

It is important to note that visa issues are common in the world of MMA and can affect both foreign fighters and events organized in foreign countries.

Promoters and fighters work to minimize these issues, but in some cases, such as Hadžović's, they can be unforeseen and unavoidable.

23

Emmanuel Yarborough is considered the heaviest fighter in UFC history and in mixed martial arts in general.

On September 9, 1994, Yarborough made his debut in the competition in a fight against Keith Hackney at UFC 3.

Yarborough weighed 616 pounds (280 kg) at that time, while Hackney weighed around 200 pounds (91 kg).

The fight lasted less than two minutes, and Hackney secured the victory with a combination of punches and leg kicks.

The significant size difference between the two fighters left a striking image in UFC history.

After his experience in the UFC, Yarborough continued to compete in other mixed martial arts events and became an advocate for the sport in the fight against obesity.

He also participated in other sports, such as judo, and even won a gold medal in judo at the 1984 Pan American Games.

24

UFC 5, which took place on April 7, 1995, in Charlotte, North Carolina, was the first UFC event to establish time limits in fights.

Prior to UFC 5, fights had no time limit and would continue until one fighter was knocked out or submitted.

This often resulted in extremely long and exhausting fights for the participants.

In UFC 5, quarterfinal and semifinal fights were set at 20 minutes each, while the final was set at 30 minutes.

However, there were no judges in the event to determine the winner in case the fight reached the end of the set time.

In the tournament final, Ken Shamrock and Royce Gracie fought for 36 minutes without a decisive result, as neither fighter was able to submit the other.

As a result, the fight was declared a draw, and both were named champions of UFC 5.

Starting from UFC 6, judges were established to prevent situations like this.

25

Bruce Buffer is an iconic presenter and announcer of UFC fights.

He made his debut at UFC 10 on July 12, 1996, and has since become an indispensable figure for the spectacle of mixed martial arts.

Buffer is known for his extravagant and energetic style when introducing the fighters before each bout, using iconic phrases like "It's time!" and "This is war!" that have become synonymous with the UFC.

He is also famous for his shout of "It's Time!" that has become his trademark. In addition to his work in the UFC, Buffer has also been a presenter at other sports events such as boxing, kickboxing, and professional wrestling.

His unique style and unmistakable voice have made him a highly popular and respected figure in the mixed martial arts community.

26

UFC 30 was a historic event for the organization as it was the first event under the ownership of the company Zuffa, led by businessmen Lorenzo and Frank Fertitta and UFC president Dana White.

Zuffa acquired the UFC in January 2001 for $2 million, rescuing it from a financial crisis and striving to establish the organization as a legitimate and respectable sport.

UFC 30 took place on February 23, 2001, at the Trump Taj Mahal in Atlantic City, New Jersey.

The event featured a showdown between two UFC legends, Mark Coleman and Pedro Rizzo, in the main event.

Coleman emerged victorious in this fight by unanimous decision after three rounds.

In addition to the main fight, the event showcased a series of other bouts, including a win by Jens Pulver over Caol Uno and a victory by Matt Hughes over Andrei Semenov.

Since then, the UFC has organized hundreds of events under the ownership of Zuffa and has grown to become one of the most successful sports organizations in the world.

27

How UFC event scheduling works.

The UFC company typically schedules multiple events in advance, with specific dates and venues.

For example, they may announce an event for the next month in Las Vegas and another event for the following month in Brazil.

However, they sometimes add additional events to the calendar on dates and venues that had not been previously announced.

In these cases, the company may make the decision to schedule an additional event based on factors such as venue availability, the popularity of fighters available to compete, and the demand from fans for more events.

Once the decision has been made to add an additional event, the company works quickly to schedule fights and promote the event so that fans have enough time to purchase tickets or subscribe to the PPV.

28

Randy Couture is considered a legend in UFC history.

On June 6, 2003, at UFC 44, he faced the reigning light heavyweight champion, Tito Ortiz.

Couture, who had previously been a heavyweight champion, achieved an impressive victory by unanimous decision and became the first fighter in UFC history to win titles in two different weight classes.

This feat earned him the nickname "The Natural" and catapulted him as one of the greatest fighters of all time.

Couture defended his light heavyweight belt twice before losing it to Vitor Belfort at UFC 46.

29

Stefan Struve, also known as "Skyscraper," is a retired Dutch fighter from the UFC.

He made his UFC debut in 2009 and throughout his career in the organization, he amassed a record of 13 wins and 11 losses.

Struve became the tallest fighter to step into the UFC octagon, standing at 2.13 meters (7 feet tall).

His reach, the measurement from the tip of one extended arm to the other, is also impressive, and he shares the record for the longest reach in the UFC with Jon Jones, both with 2.15 meters (84.5 inches).

Struve retired from the UFC in 2020 after his last fight against Ben Rothwell.

Throughout his career, Struve was known for his grappling skills and finishing opponents through submissions and knockouts.

30

UFC 100 took place on July 11, 2009, in Las Vegas and was one of the biggest events in UFC history.

In addition to the main event rematch between Frank Mir and Brock Lesnar, the event also featured a welterweight title fight between Georges St-Pierre and Thiago Alves, as well as a middleweight bout between Dan Henderson and Michael Bisping.

The event was historic in terms of pay-per-view sales, becoming the first UFC event to surpass 1.6 million buys.

It also had several noteworthy moments, such as the presence of four future UFC champions on the card, the aforementioned "Buffer 360" by Bruce Buffer, and Brock Lesnar's victory over Frank Mir in the main event.

Additionally, UFC 100 was notorious for Lesnar's controversial post-fight antics.

After defeating Mir by technical knockout in the second round, Lesnar taunted the crowd and the official UFC sponsor, Bud Light, by stating that he was going to celebrate his win by drinking Coors Light.

This controversy led to UFC losing Bud Light sponsorship for future events.

31

The fastest knockout in UFC history was achieved by Todd Duffee at UFC 102 in 2009 when he defeated Tim Hague with a powerful jab just 7 seconds into the fight.

It was an impressive victory and became one of the fastest knockouts in combat sports history.

However, there is controversy surrounding this record. UFC President Dana White announced in a press conference in 2006 that the fastest KO record in UFC belongs to Duane Ludwig, who knocked out Jonathan Goulet in just 6 seconds at UFC Fight Night 3.

White claimed that Ludwig's victory was even faster than Duffee's.

Despite this, the official record still belongs to Todd Duffee, as Ludwig's win was not officially recorded as the fastest KO due to controversy over an illegal strike that occurred during the fight.

It's important to note that, although there is controversy over the record, Todd Duffee's victory remains impressive, and he remains one of the notable fighters in the UFC.

32

Tito Ortiz is a retired American mixed martial artist (MMA) who became one of the most prominent fighters in UFC history.

Ortiz had a highly successful career in the UFC, where he was the UFC light heavyweight champion in 2000 and successfully defended the title five times.

On July 7, 2012, at UFC 148, Ortiz fought against Forrest Griffin in what would be his last fight in the UFC.

Despite losing the fight by unanimous decision, Ortiz set a record by becoming the fighter with the most fights in UFC history with 27 bouts in his record.

After his retirement, Tito Ortiz was inducted into the UFC Hall of Fame in July 2012, in recognition of his achievements in the company.

UFC President Dana White announced his induction into the Hall of Fame shortly after his last fight in the UFC, at a ceremony prior to the UFC Fan Expo event in Las Vegas.

Tito Ortiz's induction into the Hall of Fame was a recognition of his impact on the UFC and his role in popularizing MMA.

Ortiz is considered one of the pioneers of modern MMA and has been a key figure in the development of the UFC as one of the premier MMA organizations in the world.

33

UFC 151 was a mixed martial arts (MMA) event that was scheduled to take place on September 1, 2012, in Las Vegas, Nevada, but it was canceled, making it the first event to be canceled in UFC history.

The cancellation of the event was due to the injury of Dan Henderson, who was set to face light heavyweight champion Jon Jones in the main event of the card.

After Henderson's injury was announced, UFC attempted to find a replacement so that Jones could still defend his title on the lineup.

The fight was offered to Chael Sonnen, but Jones refused to accept it. With the inability to find a suitable opponent for Jones, UFC President Dana White announced at a press conference that UFC 151 would be canceled.

White was extremely disappointed with the situation and publicly criticized Jones and his training team for their refusal to accept the fight against Sonnen.

The cancellation of the event was a major blow to UFC, as the company had invested heavily in the promotion and production of the event.

Additionally, many fighters who were scheduled to compete at UFC 151 lost the opportunity to earn money and showcase themselves to the public.

Since then, UFC has implemented measures to prevent entire events from being canceled due to injuries or fighter withdrawals.

For example, the company has developed a list of backup fighters who can be called upon in case of emergencies to prevent main event fights from being canceled.

34

Anderson Silva is a retired Brazilian mixed martial artist (MMA) who was one of the most dominant fighters in the history of UFC.

In his career in the UFC, Silva established several impressive records and achievements, including a streak of 16 consecutive victories, which still stands as the company record.

On October 13, 2012, at UFC 153 in Rio de Janeiro, Brazil, Silva faced Stephan Bonnar in a light heavyweight fight.

Despite the fight being a last-minute matchup, as Bonnar was a replacement opponent, Silva did a great job in the fight and managed to win by technical knockout in the first round.

Silva's victory over Bonnar was impressive and stood out for his great technique and skill in the octagon.

The win also meant that Silva had won his 16th consecutive fight in the UFC, surpassing the previous record held by Georges St-Pierre and setting a new record for the company.

Silva's streak of consecutive victories in the UFC extended until UFC 162 in 2013, where he was surprised and defeated by challenger Chris Weidman in one of the biggest upsets in MMA history.

Despite his loss, Silva is still considered one of the greatest fighters in UFC history, and his streak of consecutive victories remains an impressive accomplishment.

35

At UFC 157, which took place on February 23, 2013, in Anaheim, California, a historic milestone occurred in the world of mixed martial arts (MMA).

For the first time in UFC history, two women fought in a main event of the company.

Ronda Rousey, the reigning Strikeforce women's bantamweight champion, faced Liz Carmouche in a fight for the inaugural UFC women's bantamweight title.

Ronda Rousey was the fan favorite in the fight and showcased her dominance in the first round.

However, Liz Carmouche managed to surprise Rousey by applying a rear-naked choke and nearly finishing the fight at that moment.

Rousey was able to defend herself and ultimately applied her famous armbar to win the fight and retain her undefeated record and the championship belt.

The Ronda Rousey vs. Liz Carmouche fight was a great success both for the UFC and for the sport in general.

It showed that women can be just as exciting and competitive as men in the octagon and opened doors for other female fighters to compete in the UFC.

Ronda Rousey became an icon in the sport and an inspiration for many women around the world.

Since then, there have been many other women's fights in the UFC, and there have been several women's bantamweight champions.

36

Fedor Emelianenko is widely regarded as one of the greatest mixed martial artists of all time.

The 6'0" (183 cm) tall, 231 lbs (105 kg) Russian fighter began his professional career in 2000 and quickly became one of the most dominant fighters of his generation.

Throughout his career, Fedor competed in various promotions, including Pride FC, Strikeforce, Affliction, and M-1 Global, but he never fought in the UFC, the world's premier MMA promotion.

Although there were some negotiations between the UFC and Fedor in the past, an agreement was never reached for him to fight in the company.

Many experts believe that the negotiations failed due to Fedor's demands regarding his salary and other contract terms.

There were also differences in the way the UFC wanted to promote Fedor.

Despite not having fought in the UFC, Fedor amassed an impressive record of 39 wins, 6 losses, and 1 draw in his career.

He is considered one of the most well-rounded and versatile fighters in history, with skills in wrestling, sambo, boxing, and Muay Thai.

His aggressive style and ability to finish his opponents made him an icon in the sport and an inspiration for many MMA fighters worldwide.

37

Emmanuel Yarborough is a retired American sumo wrestler who competed in the UFC in the 1990s.

In his debut at UFC 3 in September 1994, Yarborough faced Keith Hackney in a fight that would go down in history as one of the most lopsided in the company's history.

At the time of the fight, Yarborough weighed over 600 pounds (over 270 kilograms), making him the heaviest fighter in UFC history.

In comparison, his opponent Keith Hackney weighed only 200 pounds (less than 91 kilograms).

The significant difference in size and weight was evident from the beginning of the bout, and Hackney had to find creative ways to defend himself and attack his massive opponent.

The fight lasted less than two minutes, and although Yarborough managed to take Hackney down and keep him on the ground, his weight and size also made him vulnerable to attacks.

Hackney was able to avoid being crushed by Yarborough and eventually got rid of him, landing several strikes to win by technical knockout.

Despite his defeat at UFC 3, Emmanuel Yarborough would continue competing in sumo and other wrestling disciplines for several more years.

His size and strength made him a curious and intriguing phenomenon for many wrestling and UFC fans, but it also showed that size and weight are not always a guarantee of success in the world of mixed martial arts.

38

The fight between Conor McGregor and Khabib Nurmagomedov was one of the most anticipated in UFC history.

It took place on October 6, 2018, at the T-Mobile Arena in Las Vegas.

Khabib, the lightweight champion, defended his title against McGregor, who was returning after two years of inactivity.

Khabib defeated McGregor by submission in the fourth round and retained his title, but what happened after the fight was even more surprising.

Khabib jumped over the octagon fence and attacked McGregor's coach, Dillon Danis, while some of Khabib's teammates entered the octagon and attacked McGregor.

Meanwhile, in the stands, a member of Khabib's team jumped into the octagon and struck McGregor in the head from behind.

The fights spilled over into the seating area, and several members from both sides were arrested.

The Nevada State Athletic Commission imposed a fine of $500,000 and a nine-month suspension on Khabib, while McGregor received a fine of $50,000 and a six-month suspension.

The fight and the subsequent chaos have been considered one of the most infamous moments in UFC history.

39

The "failed" dialogue between Adesanya and the Pole.

A curious moment of the event was the "little dialogue" between Adesanya and Blachowicz with a joke from the Nigerian that, initially, led to confusion due to the language barrier.

What Adesanya said to his rival was "great guard game," but the Pole understood that, as a joke, Izzy was asking him to be his "bodyguard" and asked him, following the trick, if he "paid well."

The look of confusion on both their faces was priceless, but of course, it was all cleared up and still caused laughter for both of them.

40

Jan Blachowicz is a Polish mixed martial artist who competes in the UFC light heavyweight division.

After winning the division's title in September 2020, Blachowicz has been seeking new challenges and exciting matchups for his future in the company.

In his latest title defense, which took place in March 2021, Blachowicz faced the division's number 3 contender, Israel Adesanya, in a highly anticipated fight.

Blachowicz won the fight by unanimous decision and showcased his skills as a champion.

After the fight, Blachowicz caught the attention of many viewers and fans by pointing to Glover Teixeira, the current number 1 in the division, as his next challenge.

Teixeira had acted as a "backup" in case one of the fighters in the title bout couldn't compete, and Blachowicz seemed eager to face him in the future.

Since then, the UFC has announced that Blachowicz will fight Teixeira for the title in September 2021 in what promises to be an exciting showdown between two of the top fighters in the light heavyweight division.

Mixed martial arts fans are eager to see if Blachowicz can retain his title against the challenging Teixeira or if the Brazilian will succeed in claiming the crown.

41

After Jan Blachowicz won the UFC light heavyweight title against Dominick Reyes, there was some controversy surrounding his legitimacy as a champion.

While many believed he had earned the right to be the champion, others were still unsure if he could maintain his position as the best in the division.

After his victory against Adesanya, Blachowicz seemed to want to reaffirm his status as the champion to UFC President Dana White.

Upon receiving the championship belt, Blachowicz asked White, "Do you believe in me now?" in a reproachful tone.

White responded affirmatively, saying that he had always believed in him.

This exchange was interesting because it revealed that Blachowicz likely felt that he had not been supported enough by Dana White and the UFC prior to his victory against Adesanya.

However, White's assertion that he had always believed in him suggests that there may have been more confidence in Blachowicz than was thought.

42

Demetrious Johnson, also known as "Mighty Mouse," is considered by many as one of the greatest pound-for-pound fighters in the history of the UFC.

He excelled in the flyweight division, where he dominated for years with his technical and versatile style.

Johnson was the first-ever UFC flyweight champion and held the title for over five years.

During that time, he successfully defended the title on 11 occasions, making him the fighter with the most consecutive title defenses in UFC history.

In addition to his ability to finish opponents with submissions, Johnson also displayed great striking skills, winning several fights by technical knockout.

His fighting style was characterized by tremendous speed and agility, making him difficult to hit and predict inside the octagon.

Despite his accomplishments, some critics argue that Johnson has not received the recognition he deserves from the public, perhaps due to his lack of charisma outside the octagon.

However, for many mixed martial arts fans, his skill and consistency inside the octagon are more than enough to justify his place among the UFC greats.

43

George St-Pierre started practicing karate to defend himself against a bully in school.

Later on, he took some classes in judo and Brazilian jiu-jitsu.

Upon reaching adulthood, he worked as a garbage collector and security guard to pay for his studies.

Later, he became fascinated by mixed martial arts and turned professional.

He became the welterweight and middleweight champion.

His ability to overcome challenges, his intelligence inside the octagon, his obsession with details, studying his fights, and correcting mistakes, led him to be the dominant force in the UFC.

He is an unbeatable fighter admired by all, and at 38 years old, he is a legend of mixed martial arts.

Unlike other fighters, he despises the use of steroids in the sport to enhance performance.

He is a hardworking, consistent, and charismatic individual.

He has successfully defended his title 9 times.

44

The bonuses that fighters receive for each fight in the UFC can be quite high.

In addition to their base salary, fighters can receive a performance bonus, which is awarded to those who have an outstanding performance in their fight, whether it be an impressive finish, a dominant performance, or an exciting fight.

For example, in a typical UFC event, fighters who earn the performance bonus can receive up to $50,000 in additional dollars.

Furthermore, in special events such as championship fights, the bonuses can be even higher, reaching up to $100,000.

As for fighters' base salaries, they vary greatly depending on their level of experience and popularity.

A less relevant fighter can earn around $10,000 per fight, while more famous and successful fighters like Conor McGregor can earn much more.

In fact, McGregor has been one of the highest-paid fighters in UFC history, earning over $30 million dollars for a single fight.

It is worth mentioning that although the bonuses and salaries in the UFC can be quite high, many fighters feel that they are not adequately compensated for the risk and effort involved in training and competing at that level.

In recent years, there has been an increase in demand for better working conditions for fighters, including fairer salaries and benefits.

45

Patrick Cote: From the UFC to Badminton.

This fighter left the UFC in 2017 to pursue another sport: badminton.

Cote officially retired from the UFC in 2017 but continued his career as an MMA coach and commentator.

Cote is known for his extensive experience in mixed martial arts, having fought in the UFC from 2004 until his retirement in 2017.

During his career, Cote was a middleweight title contender and faced some of the best fighters of his time.

46

Tank Abbott is a former UFC fighter who stood out for his knockout power in the early years of the company.

In the UFC 15 event, held in October 1997, Abbott faced Hugo Duarte in a fight that lasted only 43 seconds.

Abbott landed a powerful right punch that sent Duarte to the canvas and finished the fight with a series of strikes while his opponent was on the ground.

This quick victory became one of the most memorable in UFC history.

Later on, Abbott also achieved another 43-second knockout victory, this time against Kimbo Slice in an EliteXC event in 2008.

Abbott retired from the sport in 2013 with a record of 10 wins and 15 losses in MMA.

47

Travis Fulton is a retired American fighter who holds the record for having competed in 319 fights in mixed martial arts, making him the most active fighter in the history of the sport.

He began his career in 1996 and fought in various MMA organizations, including UFC, PRIDE, and King of the Cage, among others.

Fulton has a total of 254 wins, 53 losses, and 10 draws in his career. Among his victories, 94 were by knockout and 152 by submission.

However, his career has not been without controversies, as he has been suspended on several occasions for reasons such as the use of banned substances or competing in unlicensed fights.

Despite this, Travis Fulton has been a highly respected fighter for his dedication and longevity in the sport.

His record of fights is something that is unlikely to be surpassed, making him a legend in the world of MMA.

48

Conor McGregor is a famous Mixed Martial Arts fighter from Ireland.

He was born on July 14, 1988, in Dublin, Ireland.

While it is not exactly true that he was a plumber before dedicating himself to MMA, he did work as an apprentice in that profession before his martial arts career took off.

In his youth, McGregor played football but was drawn to boxing and martial arts after watching the movie "Rocky III" as a child.

McGregor began training in mixed martial arts in 2006 and made his professional debut in 2008.

He won several regional titles before signing with the UFC in 2013. In the UFC, McGregor became a champion in two different divisions (featherweight and lightweight) and set pay-per-view sales records.

He is also known for his verbal skills and ability to promote his fights. Outside the cage, McGregor has ventured into businesses such as fashion and whiskey distillery.

In his career, McGregor has had several memorable fights, including a 13-second knockout victory over Jose Aldo in 2015 and two fights against Nate Diaz in 2016, in which each fighter won one.

He also had a highly anticipated bout against Floyd Mayweather Jr. in 2017, in which McGregor, who had never boxed professionally before, was defeated by technical knockout in the tenth round.

49

McGregor went from relying on the food assistance program to earning 60,000 euros.

When he worked as a plumber, his financial situation was very precarious.

Later on, he quit his job to fully dedicate himself to training in order to make a living from Mixed Martial Arts.

For this reason, he relied on food stamps for a while to be able to eat.

In fact, he received 188 euros per week thanks to this social assistance check.

One week later, he made his debut in a fight organized by the UFC.

His victory came by KO in the first round, and he won 60,000 dollars.

After his victory, he confessed, "I stepped into the octagon with a very clear idea: 60,000 dollars.

With this money, I can buy a car and some tailored suits." The next achievement he accomplished was renewing his contract with the UFC for a value of 100 million dollars.

50

Conor McGregor is known for being a great trash talker and using his verbal skills to unsettle his opponents and create a mental advantage before fights.

His provocative speaking style and ability to deliver quick and sharp responses have made him one of the best in the art of trash talk in the world of MMA.

Throughout his career, McGregor has engaged in several verbal confrontations with his opponents, including Nate Diaz, Jose Aldo, and Floyd Mayweather.

His provocative comments and arrogant attitude have generated both criticism and admiration among fans of the sport.

However, McGregor has also been criticized for his insults and offensive remarks, which have often crossed the line of acceptability.

Some believe that his speaking style can be counterproductive and distract him from his focus on the fight, while others see it as an integral part of his image and his success in promoting fights.

51

Aggression perpetrated by Irishman Conor McGregor, former UFC champion, against a man in a bar in Dublin, Ireland.

In the footage captured by security cameras, McGregor can be seen approaching some people at the bar and began serving them whiskey from his own brand.

One of the men, apparently older, refused to accept the invitation, and the fighter struck him in the face.

The Irish press reported that the victim was attacked after a verbal exchange, in which he reminded McGregor of his defeat last year against Russian Khabib Nurmagomedov.

The incident at the Dublin bar occurred in August 2019 and was widely publicized in the media.

After the release of the assault video, McGregor publicly apologized and claimed to be remorseful for his actions.

He also pleaded guilty to assault charges in November 2019 and was fined an undisclosed amount.

Additionally, he was suspended for six months by the Nevada State Athletic Commission for his involvement in a backstage brawl at UFC 229.

Since then, McGregor has spoken about his past behavior and claimed to be working on being a better person.

52

An incident occurred in 2019 when Conor McGregor was in Miami Beach with his family and a group of friends.

According to the complaint, a fan approached McGregor to ask for a photo with his mobile phone, but the fighter allegedly snatched the phone from the fan's hands and threw it to the ground, then proceeded to repeatedly stomp on it and take it with him.

Police were called to the scene, and after a brief search, they found McGregor at a nearby hotel and arrested him on charges of robbery and criminal mischief.

McGregor was taken to jail, and after posting a $12,500 bond, he was released.

The case was ultimately resolved in May 2019 when McGregor pleaded guilty to one count of disorderly conduct and one count of petty theft.

As part of the agreement, the fighter had to complete 50 hours of community service and pay restitution to the owner of the mobile phone in the amount of $1,000.

53

Canadian singer Drake bet $250,000 that 37-year-old fighter Jorge Masvidal would defeat Colby Covington at UFC 272, but the story in the octagon was different.

The Cuban-born fighter couldn't overcome the number one welterweight contender.

After five rounds and the same number of minutes of combat, it was Covington who raised his arms in Las Vegas, winning by unanimous decision from the judges (49-46, 50-44, and 50-45).

After the battle, in which he won the "Fight of the Night" award, Masvidal tweeted a consolation message to Drake upon learning about the fortune he had lost: "Next time you're in Miami, I'll pay for dinner," was the message received by the seven-time Grammy-winning singer.

54

Nate Diaz is a renowned American mixed martial artist who is known for his aggressive fighting style and controversial personality.

He was born on April 16, 1985, in Stockton, California, and began his MMA career in 2004.

Diaz is known for his excellent boxing and Brazilian jiu-jitsu skills, and he has competed in various weight divisions throughout his UFC career.

He is particularly famous for his rivalry with fellow fighter Conor McGregor, with whom he has had two highly anticipated and exciting fights. However, he is also known for his behavior outside the octagon.

In the past, he has been involved in several altercations with other fighters and has faced sanctions from the UFC for his behavior outside the octagon.

In 2010, he was fined by the UFC for throwing water bottles during a press conference.

In 2018, Diaz made headlines again for his behavior following the fight against McGregor at UFC 229.

Diaz and his team confronted McGregor and his team in the backstage area, which sparked a major controversy.

Despite his controversial behavior, Diaz remains one of the most popular and respected fighters in the UFC, and his exciting and aggressive fighting style has been an inspiration for many MMA fans worldwide.

55

Nate Diaz made his debut in 2007 and has competed in a total of 34 fights in his professional career.

Out of those fights, he has won 21 and lost 13.

Diaz is known for his boxing and Brazilian jiu-jitsu skills, and his specialty is submissions.

In fact, 12 of his victories have come by way of submission, showcasing his expertise on the ground.

Among his notable wins are victories over fighters such as Conor McGregor, Gray Maynard, Jim Miller, and Donald Cerrone.

He has also been recognized on multiple occasions for his impressive performances in the octagon.

However, in his most recent fight, Diaz lost to Jamaican fighter Leon 'Rocky' Edwards at UFC 263 in June 2021.

The fight was highly contested, but the judges awarded a unanimous decision in favor of Edwards.

56

How effective is Nate Diaz in his strikes?

According to data from the official UFC website, Diaz has a striking accuracy of 45%, which means he has landed 1,593 strikes out of the 3,529 strike attempts he has thrown throughout his UFC career.

This statistic highlights Diaz's ability to land strikes with precision and effectiveness, allowing him to win many fights in the octagon.

His aggressive fighting style and ability to throw accurate strikes make him a tough opponent for anyone.

It's important to note that this statistic only reflects the attempts and landed strikes in UFC fights and does not include other MMA organizations in which Diaz may have competed.

However, it still remains an important indicator of Diaz's skill and effectiveness in the fight game.

57

Justin Gaethje worked underground in a mine in his youth.

Motivated by his father (who comes from a family of miners), Gaethje began working in a mine in Morenci at the age of 18.

The work, in his own words, was extremely tough: "I worked nearly twelve hours every day, slept little, and barely ate. My record in a week was 96 hours of work."

58

Justin Gaethje suffers from both hypermetropia and myopia and wears glasses almost all the time.

Gaethje himself has said on multiple occasions that one of his major concerns when stepping into the octagon was his vision problem: "I used to be almost blind. I had terrible vision. I had 20/60 in one eye and 20/200 in the other eye. And I had hypermetropia in one eye and myopia in the other eye."

In 2016, he underwent a photorefractive keratectomy to correct his vision, and while he still experiences some difficulties in sight, he is much better now.

59

Justin Gaethje was born in North Carolina.

His mother is a Mexican-American post office director, and his father, John Ray Gaethje, as mentioned before, is a German-American miner.

He has two sisters, but the most interesting thing is that he also has a twin brother named Marcus John.

The fighter attended the University of Northern Colorado and completed a Bachelor's degree in Human Services.

He stated that he did it because he intends to do social work with at-risk youth and also because he knows that the UFC "always has an expiration date."

60

The UFC has had very few cases of fight-fixing in its history.

One of the most famous cases was at UFC 45 in 2003 when fighters Phil Baroni and Pete Sell appeared to have fixed their fight for Baroni to win.

Baroni won the fight by unanimous decision, but it was later discovered that he had bet on his own victory and had offered Sell a portion of the betting winnings if he lost.

Baroni was fined and suspended by the UFC and the Nevada State Athletic Commission.

Another case occurred at UFC 148 in 2012 when fighter Chael Sonnen was fined and suspended by the UFC and the Nevada State Athletic Commission for lying on his pre-fight drug tests for the bout against Anderson Silva.

It was discovered that Sonnen had lied about his use of testosterone replacement therapy and had tested positive in a post-fight test.

Overall, the UFC has strict policies and procedures in place to prevent fight-fixing and takes any suspicion or accusation of fixing very seriously.

The integrity of the fights is essential to the reputation and ongoing success of the UFC.

61

Justin Gaethje took his first steps in the sport of wrestling when he was only 3 years old.

His father encouraged him to participate in sports to enhance his motor skills.

Later, at Safford High School, he continued to improve: he still holds the seventh-closest falls record (218) and the ninth-highest team points (1057.5) in the state's wrestling history.

62

Fouls inside the octagon:

1. Headbutts.
2. Any eye gouging.
3. Biting.
4. Spitting at an opponent.
5. Pulling hair.
6. Fish hooking (putting a finger inside an opponent's mouth and pulling to the side).
7. Any type of attack to the groin.
8. Putting a finger into any orifice, cut, or laceration of an opponent.
9. Small joint manipulation.
10. Striking downward with the point of the elbow.
11. Strikes to the spine or the back of the head.
12. Heel kicking the liver.
13. Strikes of any kind to the throat.
14. Grabbing, pinching, or twisting the skin.
15. Grabbing the clavicle.
16. Kicking the head of a grounded opponent.
17. Knee striking the head of a grounded opponent.
18. Stomping a grounded opponent.
19. Grabbing the fence.
20. Grabbing an opponent's shorts or gloves.
21. Using obscene language inside the ring/fighting area.
22. Unsportsmanlike conduct that causes injury to an opponent.
23. Attacking an opponent during a break.
24. Attacking an opponent being attended to by the referee.
25. Attacking an opponent after the bell signaling the end of the round.
26. Timidity, including, without limits, avoiding contact with an opponent intentionally or repeatedly spitting out the mouthguard or feigning an injury.
27. Throwing an opponent out of the ring/fighting area.
28. Intentionally not obeying the referee's instructions.
29. Slamming an opponent to the ground on their head or neck.
30. Interfering in the corner.
31. Applying any foreign substance to the hair or body to gain an advantage.

63

Santiago Ponzinibbio: adversities and uncertainties he experienced in Brazil.

Despite being a Top 10 fighter in his welterweight category, the native of La Plata didn't have an easy path.

In an interview with Infobae, he recounted his story and talked about the possibility of facing the company's most popular fighter, Conor McGregor.

"I used to play rugby. From a young age, I liked contact sports, and once I went to a gym for physical conditioning with recreational Muay Thai classes, and I was fascinated. They had me hitting the bag like crazy, and I started going there to train," Santiago Ponzinibbio said about his first encounter with martial arts at the age of 15.

A boxer friend taught him the techniques, while another friend, a bodybuilder, provided him with nutrition plans.

"It was all very new," admits the fighter. "I won many fights, and with each one, I got more excited until I said, 'Well, I'm going somewhere to seek knowledge. There were teams in Buenos Aires, but there was no level, so I went to Brazil."

64

Santiago Ponzinibbio had made a difficult decision to leave the country at the age of 20, but the 7 years he lived there were even tougher.

"I left with nothing, just two shirts and two pants. A friend paid for my bus ticket, and we went to a tent in a campground. From there, I went to the beach to find someone wearing a Jiu-Jitsu shirt and ask them where they trained. That's how the utopian journey began."

65

Santiago Ponzinibbio commented:

"At first, I had to pay my dues. I encountered two or three people who took advantage of me. They thought I had money and ignored me. Until one day, I met a guy who started giving me cool classes, and that's when I went out to look for work to be able to pay for them, doing whatever it took to earn money," details the Argentine who went through various jobs, from being a masseur to selling breaded cutlets on the beach.

66

Santiago Ponzinibbio spent 7 years in Brazilian lands, and regarding his training in this country, he comments, "It was difficult, they hit me quite a bit, and they didn't want to teach me because I was Argentine. But they saw that I was tough and kept pushing, so they ended up teaching me."

67

At the moment when Ponzinibbio held a record of 18-1 (with one "slightly controversial" loss), it seemed that his sacrifice had paid off, as he received the opportunity to enter the UFC reality show, The Ultimate Fighter in Rio de Janeiro.

However, a new obstacle presented itself: "I bought the ticket, and when I arrived, they told me I couldn't participate because I was Argentine.

The idea of that tournament was to reveal talents from that country, and the production company had doubts about me.

They didn't want to include people from other countries." Nevertheless, Santiago was persistent, he told his story and justified that he had been living in Brazil for years.

"In the end, they called me and said I could enter. When I received that call, a weight was lifted off my shoulders. At that point, it all depended on me."

The native of La Plata made an impression, becoming one of the 16 qualifiers out of the 550 applicants.

However, as he advanced in the reality show, the criticism from the public increased.

"I was the surprise of the program. My entry caused a lot of controversy because they said, 'No, an Argentine cannot participate. He is taking the spot away from one of ours.'"

The Argentinean defeated Brazilians one by one until reaching the semifinals. There, a new setback was about to hit him: "At the beginning of the fight, after two minutes, I broke my arm. Every time I threw a right punch, my wrist would bend as if it were made of rubber."

He managed to finish the fight and won by the judges' decision, despite having broken his radius in 10 parts since the beginning.

Santiago said goodbye to the final, but news came at the worst moment and changed his life: "UFC gave me the contract, a bonus for that fight, and one for the best knockout."

In 2013, Santiago Ponzinibbio signed with the world's premier mixed martial arts organization.

68

What does Ponzinibbio think seconds before the bell rings for the first round?

"That I'm going to have fun and give everything I have, as always. Give more than my 100% when fighting and enjoy every moment because it goes by very quickly. It's only 15/25 minutes up there. This is what I love to do, I'm very happy doing this."

69

Chael Sonnen is a former American mixed martial artist (MMA) who stood out for his wrestling skills and controversial personality in the world of MMA.

During his career in the UFC, Sonnen had several memorable moments, one of which was the shout of "don't touch me!" This shout originated in a pre-fight press conference between Sonnen and Brazilian fighter Wanderlei Silva.

During the conference, Silva approached Sonnen to try to intimidate him, and Sonnen shouted "don't touch me!" as a joke to provoke his opponent and make the audience laugh.

However, this shout was already known to UFC fans years before when Sonnen shouted it in protest after losing his title shot against then-champion Anderson Silva at UFC 148.

At that moment, Sonnen complained about a rib injury and refused to let Anderson Silva touch him during the winner announcement ceremony, leading to a tense and confusing situation in the octagon.

Although the shout of "don't touch me!" originated in a tense situation, Sonnen has since used it as a joke in press conferences and as a way to provoke his opponents and entertain the audience.

70

After his defeat at UFC 98 against Frankie Edgar, Sean Sherk was seen leaving the MGM Grand Garden Arena in Las Vegas running shirtless with his shorts and gloves still on.

When asked about the incident, Sherk stated that he was so angry about losing that he decided to "go for a little run" to relax.

It took him a little over an hour to return.

71

UFC events have taken place in the USA, Canada, Ireland, Brazil, Germany, England, Australia, Japan, Puerto Rico, and the United Arab Emirates.

With at least one event per month, there are several opportunities to watch an event on TV or online.

72

The octagon is the regular octagon-shaped structure used in mixed martial arts (MMA) events of the UFC, and it has become one of the most recognized features of the sport.

The main reason an octagon is used instead of a ring in the UFC is, in fact, for safety purposes.

In a traditional ring, fighters can fall or be thrown out of it, which can result in serious injuries.

The octagon, on the other hand, has a safer structure that helps keep the fighters within the competition area.

The regular octagon-shaped structure helps prevent injuries as fighters cannot be thrown out of the fighting area, and the rounded corners of the octagon help prevent head injuries.

Additionally, the octagon also has a specific size and shape that are designed to create a fair and balanced environment for competition.

The size of the octagon is 30 feet in diameter, providing enough space for fighters to move and work, but it is not so large as to make the fight boring or difficult to follow for spectators.

73

In mixed martial arts (MMA), including the UFC, a championship fight lasts for 5 rounds of 5 minutes each.

This applies to all championships, including lightweight, welterweight, middleweight, light heavyweight, and heavyweight titles.

On the other hand, regular fights that are not for a title have a duration of 3 rounds of 5 minutes each.

This applies to all weight categories and is the standard duration of a fight in the UFC.

It is important to note that rounds in MMA are divided into rounds, and each round has a duration of 5 minutes.

Between each round, fighters have a 1-minute break to recover and receive instructions from their coaches.

In some cases, fights may end before the scheduled time due to knockout, submission, or technical decision.

If this occurs in a championship fight, the winning fighter becomes the champion or retains their title, while in a regular fight, the winning fighter secures the victory but not a title.

74

Khabib Nurmagomedov is a retired Russian mixed martial artist (MMA) who retired in October 2020 with an impressive undefeated record of 29 wins and no losses.

He is considered one of the greatest fighters in UFC history, especially in the lightweight division.

Born in Dagestan, Russia, Khabib grew up in a family of wrestlers and began training in sambo and wrestling at a young age.

In 2008, he made his professional MMA debut and won his first 16 fights outside of the UFC.

In 2012, Khabib signed with the UFC and quickly proved to be a formidable fighter with his impressive grappling ability and his knack for controlling his opponents on the ground.

In April 2018, he won the UFC lightweight title by defeating the then-champion, Al Iaquinta.

Throughout his career, Khabib gained fame for his relentless and dominant fighting style, as well as his humility and respect outside the octagon.

He is also known for his close relationship with his father and coach, Abdulmanap Nurmagomedov, who passed away in 2020 due to COVID-19-related complications.

Khabib's last fight in the UFC was in October 2020 when he defeated Justin Gaethje by submission in the second round.

After the fight, Khabib announced his retirement from the sport and cited his father's death as one of the main reasons for his decision.

75

Anderson Silva is considered one of the greatest fighters in the history of mixed martial arts (MMA) and one of the most dominant ones.

The Brazilian fighter holds the record for the most title defenses in the UFC, with a total of 10 consecutive title defenses in the middleweight division, from 2006 to 2013.

This record surpasses any other UFC champion in any weight category. On the other hand, Randy Couture is also one of the most successful fighters in the UFC.

The American has been a champion in two different weight divisions, heavyweight and light heavyweight.

Couture also holds the record for having fought in 15 UFC title fights, a number that no other fighter has matched.

Couture is a pioneer in MMA and has been a role model for many UFC fighters.

He is also known for his dedication and his ability to adapt to different fighting styles.

Winning two championship belts in two different weight categories is an impressive achievement and showcases Couture's versatility and skill as a fighter.

76

The fight between Stephan Bonnar and Forrest Griffin in the light heavyweight final of the first season of The Ultimate Fighter was considered a pivotal moment in UFC history.

The fight took place in April 2005 and became an instant classic due to its intensity and excitement.

The fight was highly competitive, and both fighters gave their all during the three rounds.

After the fight, Dana White, the president of the UFC, offered contracts to both fighters, allowing them to continue their careers in the UFC.

The fight is often cited as a turning point in the popularity of the UFC and is considered one of the greatest fights in MMA history.

77

Cutmen are assigned to the red or blue corners by the event organizers and are not chosen by the fighters.

Cutmen are responsible for tending to the fighters' wounds and cuts between rounds and ensuring that the fighters are in the best possible condition to continue the fight.

Cutmen are highly trained professionals who use special techniques to stop bleeding and reduce swelling in injured areas.

They often have experience in sports medicine and have worked with many MMA fighters in the past.

It is worth noting that some fighters also bring their own personal cutman to fights if they have a close working relationship and trust that person's skills.

However, the event organizer still assigns the official cutmen to each corner.

78

Are there people outside of the competition who can defeat a UFC fighter?

Most likely yes, but it would depend on the context, as if you take a fighter out of the octagon and the rules of the UFC, they are outside of their habitat, and therefore it would not be a very comfortable fight and they would have significant disadvantages, such as in a freestyle fight.

But if we assume it's a fight inside the octagon with the rules of the UFC, there is the case of Mirko "Cro Cop" Filipovic, who never fought in the UFC but was an undefeated champion for 10 years in PRIDE and Affliction.

79

Why do UFC fighters keep throwing punches or elbows when their opponents have already been knocked out?

No one can stop them at that moment because they are filled with adrenaline.

They are in a primal survival state of mind during the fight, completely focused on winning.

They only react and don't think about whether someone is okay or not.

They have an opportunity and they take it without thinking about anything else.

One of the functions of the referee is to ensure the safety of the fighters.

80

What has been the shortest UFC fight?

The fight literally lasted 4 seconds, after which the fighter was knocked out on the ground.

Jorge Masvidal, also known as "Street Jesus," is a fighter of Cuban and Peruvian descent.

At UFC 239, he fought against Ben Askren.

As the fight approached, Askren took to the media to mock Masvidal's religion and Cuban heritage, something that didn't sit well with him.

On the day of the highly anticipated fight, Askren was in his corner, and Masvidal in the other.

The referee shouted "FIGHT," and suddenly Masvidal sprinted forward, jumped, and delivered a powerful knee strike that rendered Askren unconscious just 4 seconds into the fight, achieving the fastest KO in UFC history.

81

Why was UFC fighter Conor McGregor unbeatable until he suddenly started losing fights and having issues with his opponents?

Although Royce Gracie or Dan Severn have nothing directly to do with McGregor, there was a time when Gracie was unbeatable, and Brazilian Jiu-Jitsu was considered the most dominant martial art.

Gracie weighed around 180 pounds (81 kg) and yet defeated Severn, who weighed 260 pounds (117 kg).

Gracie was dominated by Matt Hughes in UFC 60, and none of his previous invincibility techniques were effective in that fight.

What had changed?

Matt Hughes was clearly a high-quality opponent who knew what he was doing and had made the necessary adjustments to neutralize Gracie's Jiu-Jitsu.

Similarly, current UFC fighters would have studied McGregor's footage, identified his strengths and weaknesses, and made appropriate adjustments.

When McGregor fought Khabib, he himself was dominated and realized what happens when facing a high-quality opponent because techniques that work against certain mid-range fighters do not work against the best.

Additionally, in McGregor's specific case, the aging process and motivational issues contributed significantly to his rapid decline.

82

What is the difference between UFC and MMA?

UFC stands for Ultimate Fighting Championship. It is the equivalent of the NBA for basketball or FIFA for soccer.

MMA stands for Mixed Martial Arts, which means in the UFC, they are searching for the best in MMA.

MMA is a combat sport that combines different disciplines of martial arts, such as boxing, kickboxing, jiu-jitsu, wrestling, and more.

The UFC focuses on promoting high-level MMA fights and growing the sport worldwide.

83

In the early days, the combat style that showed more dominance over others was Brazilian Jiu-Jitsu.

Another style is Wrestling, in all its forms, including Olympic, Greco-Roman, freestyle, etc.

This is because it has been observed that when you match up a good stand-up fighter in boxing, kickboxing, muay thai, etc., with a specialist in ground fighting like Jiu-Jitsu or Wrestling, most of the time the Jiu-Jitsu and/or Wrestling fighter wins the fight.

That doesn't mean these styles are invincible, but they have certain advantages over others.

However, it also doesn't mean that a stand-up specialist cannot defeat a ground-fighting specialist.

The most successful strategy seen in these matchups is for the stand-up specialist to practice their takedown defense because if they successfully defend takedown attempts and keep the fight standing, they are more likely to win the fight.

84

Rousimar Palhares is a former Brazilian mixed martial artist who gained a bad reputation in the UFC due to his unsportsmanlike and dangerous behavior in the octagon.

Palhares was known for holding onto his submissions even after his opponents had tapped, leading to several of them suffering unnecessary injuries.

One of the most infamous cases of this behavior occurred at UFC Fight Night 29 when Palhares defeated Mike Pierce by submission.

After Pierce tapped out, Palhares continued to hold the heel hook for several seconds, causing an ankle injury that required Pierce to undergo surgery.

The UFC sanctioned Palhares for this behavior and temporarily suspended him.

However, Palhares continued with his unsportsmanlike conduct in his next fight, where he again held a submission after his opponent had tapped.

Due to this repeated inappropriate behavior, the UFC decided to permanently release him from the organization in 2015.

Since then, Palhares has continued to compete in other MMA promotions, although he has continued to receive criticism for his unsportsmanlike behavior in the octagon.

85

A spectacular night of knockouts and adrenaline was experienced at the UFC Apex in Florida with the UFC 250 event, where Brazilian champion Amanda Nunes made history by becoming the first titleholder to defend both of her titles, successfully defending the featherweight championship against Canadian challenger Felicia Spencer.

The main event of UFC 250 left no room for surprises as Amanda Nunes easily defeated challenger Felicia Spencer.

From the first round, the champion unleashed her famous power strikes on the Canadian, who did her best to withstand the onslaught from the "Lioness."

In the following rounds, Spencer's strategy shifted to attempting takedowns, but Amanda used her Jiu-Jitsu to punish her opponent on the ground, even causing a significant lump on Felicia's forehead, which could have led to the fight being stopped.

The fight remained unchanged for the final rounds, and after an attempted submission and more strikes to Spencer's face, the fight ended with a unanimous decision victory for the reigning champion, who celebrated with the triumph of both her Bantamweight and Featherweight titles.

86

Herb Dean is one of the most recognized and respected referees in the UFC, but before his career as a referee, he also had a career as a professional mixed martial artist.

Dean competed in various organizations, including the UFC, and had a record of 2 wins and 3 losses before retiring in 2007.

One of his notable fights was against fellow former UFC fighter Joe Riggs at the WEC 10 event in 2003, where Dean lost by technical knockout in the first round.

Despite his struggles as a fighter, Herb Dean is best known for his work as a referee, where he has been recognized for his ability to keep fighters safe during fights and for making fair and impartial decisions in combat situations.

87

Ronda Rousey was the first female UFC champion in the bantamweight division and opened the doors for women in the UFC in 2012.

Prior to her arrival, the UFC did not have female divisions, and White had stated that he had no plans to create one.

But Rousey changed all of that with her impressive career, winning her first 6 UFC fights by first-round submission and becoming one of the biggest and most popular stars in the organization.

Her success led to the creation of more female divisions, including featherweight and flyweight.

Rousey was also a great advocate for women's sports and women's empowerment in general.

88

Ronda Rousey was known for her ability to quickly finish her opponents in the UFC cage, with an average fight duration of around 3 minutes.

In fact, 9 of her 12 UFC victories came in the first round, many of them within the first few minutes of the fight.

Her fastest time record was in her fight against Cat Zingano at UFC 184, when she submitted her in just 14 seconds with her famous armbar.

This ability to quickly finish her opponents made her one of the most feared and dominant fighters of her time.

89

Ronda Rousey's signature move is a grappling technique called an "armbar," which involves applying pressure on the opponent's elbow or shoulder joint to force a submission or cause an injury.

It is one of the most effective and commonly used moves in mixed martial arts, and Rousey stood out for her ability to apply it with precision and speed in the octagon.

In fact, out of her 12 professional MMA victories, 9 were by submission, primarily through this technique.

Rousey has also showcased her expertise in the armbar in judo competitions, where she won a bronze medal at the 2008 Beijing Olympics.

90

The UFC fighters who have earned the most money in their careers.

–Conor McGregor: The Irish fighter is undoubtedly the highest-earning athlete in UFC history, thanks to his skills inside the octagon and his personality outside of it. McGregor has earned an estimated $180 million in his UFC career.

–Khabib Nurmagomedov: The Russian fighter, who retired in 2020, had an impressive career in the UFC with an undefeated record of 29-0. Although not as well-known as McGregor outside the octagon, Nurmagomedov has earned a significant amount of money in his career, with an estimated $30 million.

–Georges St-Pierre: The former welterweight and middleweight champion of the UFC, St-Pierre is considered by many as one of the greatest fighters of all time. Throughout his career, he earned an estimated $20 million in the UFC.

–Brock Lesnar: The professional wrestler and former heavyweight champion of the UFC, Lesnar has been one of the most prominent fighters in UFC history. Despite fighting in the UFC for a relatively short period, he earned an estimated $16 million in his career.

–Anderson Silva: The former middleweight champion of the UFC, Silva is known for his unique fighting style and his ability to finish his opponents quickly. Throughout his UFC career, he earned an estimated $14 million.

91

She contemplated suicide after her first loss.

Fighter Ronda Rousey surprised all her loyal fans and mixed martial arts enthusiasts when she confessed in an interview with Ellen DeGeneres that she considered taking her own life after her unexpected first loss.

"I thought about killing myself," Rousey said with tears in her eyes.

"In that exact second, I'm like, I'm nothing, what do I do anymore? No one gives a shit about me."

Ronda Rousey's first loss in the UFC was against Holly Holm at UFC 193 on November 14, 2015.

Holm won the fight by knockout in the second round after landing a high kick to Rousey's head.

92

The reign of Dana White.

Dana White became the president of the UFC in 2001 and has since been a key figure in the popularization and success of the company.

One of his main achievements has been turning the UFC into a mass spectator sport, using various strategies to attract a wider audience.

Among the strategies that Dana White has employed to promote the UFC are creating rivalries and fights with a strong emotional charge, producing documentaries and TV programs about the fighters and the sport, and using social media to generate hype before events.

Additionally, White has also been a strong advocate for transparency in anti-doping test results and has worked to eradicate the use of illegal substances in the UFC.

Thanks to his vision and innovative strategies, the UFC has become a global phenomenon and has generated a significant amount of revenue through pay-per-view and sponsorships.

93

Born in the Republic of Dagestan on September 20, 1988, Khabib Nurmagomedov lived in one of the areas most affected by terrorism in Russia.

In that area, he forged his character from a young age, thanks to his father Abdulmanap, a former Soviet Union military.

Unlike other children, Khabib showed interest in wrestling.

This is because his father trained young people to join the national team in that discipline, but his first challenge would come at the age of 9.

It was September 23, 1997, Khabib had already celebrated his birthday, but his father had a surprise for him.

When he went out into the street, he realized that his gift was a bear, almost his size.

Khabib didn't have a better idea than to fight the bear.

Immediately, his father grabbed the camcorder and started filming the encounter.

"A child always wants to show his father what he is capable of. What I saw was a test of character," Abdulmanap confessed years later in an interview.

94

Welterweight fighter Jordan Williams was shopping at a gas station in Colorado when he noticed a man trying to steal his car.

His reaction was priceless.

The 30-year-old American quickly ran to intervene: he opened the door and took him down with knee strikes.

To top it off, the thief left his cap inside the vehicle, and Williams uploaded a photo to his social media with the message:

"Forgot your cap?"

95

Although Nate Diaz, along with his brother, fellow fighter Nick Diaz, is known for the quality of their strikes and everything they have achieved in their combat sports careers, they are also recognized for their love of marijuana whenever they can.

Among the various controversial episodes surrounding the younger of the Diaz brothers, there is one that he experienced in 2016 when he appeared with a CBD vaporizer at the press conference following his victory over his arch-rival, Conor McGregor.

On that occasion, he explained the benefits he felt from using it, as he believed it greatly helped him in the process of recovering from the blows he received.

The episode did not go unnoticed by the top management of the UFC, who instead of suspending him issued a public warning.

However, when the United States Anti-Doping Agency removed marijuana from its list of prohibited substances, the Californian fighter showed up before his fight with Englishman Leon Edwards at UFC 278, smoking a cannabis cigarette.

96

For some time now, Diaz has been well known for his dissatisfaction with the UFC management, primarily with its president, Dana White, largely due to the lack of financial benefits he has received from the organization, as well as the diminished spotlight given to him in recent years.

Tensions between both parties were such that on one occasion, the American took the opportunity to stage a controversial protest at the UFC headquarters.

On May 12th, Diaz posted a message on his Twitter account, accompanied by an image showing him urinating outside the UFC PI.

"Pissing on the UFC PI. I can do this because they pay me more than all the guys, and they won't cut me," Diaz wrote in the post's description.

97

In UFC 196, held on March 5, 2016, Nate Diaz faced Conor McGregor and returned the blow of defeat he suffered in their first encounter.

Among the explanations he provided about what had changed in relation to the previous fight, the American highlighted that the change in his diet was crucial to the outcome.

For over a decade, the Diaz brothers have stopped eating meat and consuming dairy, adopting a vegan diet.

"Who's the real caveman here? Eating what comes from the earth is the most natural thing there is. Eating something that comes from animals only makes you heavier. I think the smartest thing to do is to change the diet to something more organic," he stated at the time in response to the Irishman's provocations.

98

Offering Free Fights.

Marlon Chito Vera is an Ecuadorian fighter in the UFC's bantamweight division.

Before joining the UFC, Vera had a career in various mixed martial arts promoters, especially in his home country, Ecuador.

During that time, it is said that Vera offered free fights to Latin promoters so they could see his talent and possibly sign him.

This unconventional marketing strategy helped him make a name for himself in the regional MMA scene and eventually led him to the UFC, where he has found success and become one of the top contenders in his division.

99

The Consistency of a Champion.

Daniel Cormier is a special case in the UFC, as he is one of the few fighters who has simultaneously held titles in two different divisions: light heavyweight and heavyweight.

And he achieved this as a professional in the UFC at the age of 30.

He is the epitome of a consistent, hardworking, dedicated, and disciplined athlete who reaches the highest level thanks to his work and dedication.

Additionally, he possesses an extraordinary quality for a contact sport: he can take punches very well, he is tough as a rock.

His career is nearly flawless: 22-1.

His only loss came against his greatest rival, both inside and outside the octagon: Jon Jones.

However, despite the confrontations and exchange of words with this fighter, Cormier is an example outside the cage, a patient and diplomatic person.

Life tested him when his young daughter passed away in a car accident.

100

Alexander "The Great" Volkanovski is one of the most talented Australian UFC fighters in the country's history.

As a featherweight champion, he was previously a semi-professional Rugby player in his country.

It was only when he started training in MMA and Greco-Roman wrestling that he found his true passion and focus on a professional career as a fighter.

His nickname "The Great" is based on King Alexander III of Macedonia.

The king is known for his conquest of the Persian Empire, which earned him the title Alexander The Great.

Alexander was a semi-professional Rugby player with the Warilla Gorillas in the Australian Rugby League, where he won the Mick Cronin Medal and the premier league.

Volkanovski has earned over a million dollars in the UFC, receiving the attractive sum of $390,000 USD for his rematch with Max Holloway.

His net worth is estimated to be above $2 million dollars.

101

Basic Requirements to Enter the Ultimate Fighter:

-Be available for the date of the qualifying trials in the chosen city (usually Las Vegas, Nevada, USA). Applicants will be required to perform grappling and pad striking and must bring appropriate MMA equipment.

-The fighter must have a minimum of 3 professional MMA fights in their experience to be considered. All records will be verified. If we cannot verify the record on online sites such as Sherdog and Mixedmartialarts.com, the applicant will not be eligible for the selection.

-Applicants must be between the ages of 21 and 34 and have the legal ability to live and work in the United States.

-If not a U.S. citizen, the applicant must obtain a criminal background report from an authorized organization in their country of residence and submit the report.

-All applicants must complete and sign the application form and bring it to the trials. Applicants will be notified at the end of the trials if they have been selected to participate in the final casting process. If selected, applicants must be prepared to stay in the chosen city for the show.

We hope you enjoyed reading the book.

If you found the information interesting,
we would like to ask you a favor.

It would be of great help if you could take a
few minutes to leave a review on Amazon.

Your opinion is very valuable to us and other
readers who are looking for information
about the UFC.

Your review will also help us improve our work
and continue creating content that
is of interest.

We know that the process of leaving a review
can be a bit cumbersome, but if you feel
comfortable doing so, we would
be very grateful.

Thank you for your support!